AEROPLANES IN COLOUR

First published 1976.

ISBN 07110 6709 8

Front cover: Two early examples of the Blackburn (now Hawker Siddeley) Buccaneer naval strike aircraft, capable of carrying nuclear and conventional weapons, on test.   *Hawker Siddeley Aviation*

Back cover, upper: Boeing 747-31 N91307 of Trans World Airlines leaves the jumbo jet terminal at Heathrow Airport in 1970.   *A. T. Halse,*
Aviation Photo News

Back cover, lower: The South-Western Electricity Board's first helicopter, Agusta-Bell 47J-2 G-ASLR, lands at Bristol/Lulsgate in December 1971.
Peter R. March

PUBLISHED BY
IAN ALLAN LTD
TERMINAL HOUSE·SHEPPERTON·TW17 8AS·ENGLAND
TELEPHONE: WALTON-ON-THAMES 28484

Printed by Crampton & Sons Ltd, Sawston, Cambridge

In this book we present a collection of colour pictures of aircraft representing over 60 years of development of the flying machine.   All of the pictures have been published before in Ian Allan magazines or books but we make no apology for reproducing them again since they have made possible this lively pictorial gathering of old and new aeroplanes in a variety of liveries and roles in inexpensive book form. Many of the better-known military aircraft are represented, from a World War I Zeppelin-killing Sopwith Camel through the British and German stalwarts of World War II, the Spitfire and Messerschmitt, to the Vulcans, Lightnings and Phantoms of today's air forces.   The ubiquitous and multi-purpose helicopter, the smaller general-purpose aircraft, the now commonplace monstrous Boeing 747 and the ultimate in supersonic transport, the brilliant and controversial Concorde, all help to make up this fascinating kaleidoscope of 20th-century aeronautical achievement.

The Avro 504K trainer—one of the few survivors of the world-famous Avro 504 marque—revs up for take-off at Old Warden aerodrome, Beds, home of the Shuttleworth Collection of historic aircraft.

A gaily decorated Fokker DVII gets ready to take part in a World War I-style dogfight at the Old Rhinebeck Aerodrome, New York, in 1967. *Peter Kilduff*

Above: Lt Culley's Zeppelin-killing Sopwith Camel fighter of World War I in its present home, the Imperial War Museum at Lambeth. *Stuart Howe*

Below: Hawker Typhoon IB MN235 of the RAF Museum collection pictured at 27 MU, Shawbury, Salop, in 1970. *Paul Terian*

The Hawker Hart II which was originally Hawker's demonstration and, later, 'hack' Hart, G-ABMR, on show at RAF Cranwell, Lincs, in June 1970. Painted to represent a machine of B Flight of 57 (Bomber) Squadron, it is today preserved in the RAF Museum at Hendon. *Aviation Photo News*

Left: Hawker Hurricane IIC LS363 of the RAF's Battle of Britain Memorial Flight flies over the East Yorkshire countryside in 1969 on its way home to RAF Coltishall, Norfolk, after taking part in an air display in Scotland. *Peter Sargent*

Below left: Showpiece in front of SHQ at RAF Coltishall is this Spitfire 16, SL542, in front of which is displayed a nameplate and plaque from the old SR Battle of Britain class Pacific locomotive No 34066 *Spitfire.* *Stuart Howe*

Above: Spitfire PR19 PM631 from the Battle of Britain Memorial Flight at RAF Coltishall crosses the Kent Coast near Ramsgate. *Peter Sargent*

Below: Messerschmitt Bf 109G-2 Werke Nummer 10639 pictured at RAF Coltishall after restoration to represent Yellow 14 of JG53 'Pik As'. *Aviation Photo News*

The navigator of Boeing B-17F 230721 *Sweet and Lovely* of the 381st Bomb Group (Heavy), US 8th Air Force, puts his flight bag on a crew truck at Ridgewell, Essex, after a World War II bombing mission while the captain writes a report. *USAF Official*

Contact! CASA 2.111 (Spanish licence-built version of the wartime Heinkel 111 H-16) has an engine test at Bovingdon, Herts, in September 1968 when aircraft used in the 'Battle of Britain' film were displayed to the press. *Richard Riding*

A vic of McDonnell Douglas Phantom FG1s of 43
Squadron RAF, on detachment to RAF Luqa, Malta,
flying over the Mediterranean during Exercise Lime
Jug in the autumn of 1970. *Ministry of Defence*

The Fleet Air Arm Museum's veteran Fairey
Swordfish LS326 displays its purposeful lines at an air
show at Elstree aerodrome in June 1966.   *N. B. Rivett*

Left: Avro Vulcan B2 XM647 of the Near East Air
Force Bomber Wing flies over the glistening
Mediterranean during a sortie from its base at Akrotiri,
Cyprus, in July 1969.   *Ministry of Defence*

Above: Avro Shackleton MR3 WR981 of 120
Squadron, Coastal Command, on a sortie from RAF
Kinloss.   *Hawker Siddeley Aviation*

Above: LTV A-7E Corsair II 157454 311 of VA133 Squadron—'The Stingers'—from USS *Ranger* pictured at NAS Le Moore in May 1970.   *Aviation Photo News*

Below: The seventh pre-production Westland Wyvern TF1, VR137, photographed at the Fleet Air Arm Museum at RNAS Yeovilton in 1969. *Stuart Howe*

Above: Colourful Cat. Consolidated Catalina water-bomber N6453C in the air at Burbank, California, in September 1970. *Aviation Photo News*

Below: Grumman US-2C Tracker 133359 of US Navy Squadron VC4 Detachment at Cecil Field, Florida, in 1967. *Aviation Photo News*

Above: Fiat G-91R3 31+88 of Le KG41, Federal German Air Force, pictured while attending RAF Chivenor's NATO Air Day in 1969.
Aviation Photo News

Below: Convair F-102A Delta Dagger 061006 of the 178th FIS—'The Happy Hooligans'—North Dakota Air Guard, at Fargo, North Dakota, in July 1968.
Aviation Photo News

Above: The famous North American F-100D-65-NA
63000 *Triple Zilch* of the 55th TFS/20th TFW visiting
RAF Wattisham in September 1957. *B. A. Forward*

Below: McDonnell Douglas A-4E Skyhawk 152031
of VA-94, USS *Bon Homme Richard*, pictured at North
Island NAS in March 1969. *Aviation Photo News*

Above: McDonnell Douglas F-4J Phantom 153779 of VF84 from USS *Independence* pictured at Offut AFB, Nebraska, in June 1967. *Aviation Photo News*

Below: McDonnell Douglas F-4D Phantom 50769 of the 10th TFS, 50th TFW, USAF, at Spangdahlem, Germany. *Aviation Photo News*

Above: English Electric P1A 7755M ex-WG760, the prototype of the Lightning, seen at RAF Henlow in November 1970. *Stuart Howe*

Below: An all-yellow Gloster Meteor NF14 night fighter used as a chase plane by the Aeroplane & Armament Experimental Establishment at Boscombe Down, Wilts. *Aviation Photo News*

Drink-up chaps!   Two McDonnell Douglas Phantom
FG1s of 43 Squadron, 'The Fighting Cocks', refuel
from a Handley Page Victor K1 tanker of 57 Squadron.
Ministry of Defence

Lockheed F-80B Shooting Stars of the USAF's
famous 'Hat in the Ring' Squadron, the 94th FS,
flying in formation during a sortie from March Field,
California, in late 1947. *Lockheed*

Above: One of 46 Squadron's Hawker Siddeley Andover C1s (XS639) sporting on its fin the unit's badge comprising three red arrowheads, a device first seen on the unit's pre-war Gloster Gauntlet fighters. *Aviation Photo News*

Below: Lockheed Hercules C1 XV298 visits Prestwick for a Royal Air Forces Association display in late 1966. *J. M. Friell via Aviation Photo News*

Right: 114 Squadron Armstrong Whitworth Argosy C1 XR109 over the outskirts of Wallingford, Oxon, whose coat of arms is carried on its nose. *Peter R. March*

Right below: De Havilland Chipmunk WG316, one of the first of its type to appear in the new red, white and grey colour scheme of RAF Training Command in 1971. *Adrian M. Balch*

Folland Gnat T1 XP506 of 4 FTS streaks past South Stack lighthouse, Holyhead, during a low-flying sortie from its base at Valley, Anglesey, in 1971.
Ministry of Defence

Above: Hawker Siddeley Dominie T1 XS730 H of 6 FTS, Finningley, Yorks, seen at RAF Biggin Hill's Battle of Britain display in September 1970.
Aviation Photo News

Below: De Havilland Chipmunk T10 WZ873 E of London University Air Squadron pictured at Biggin Hill in September 1970. *Aviation Photo News*

Canadian Armed Forces Lockheed C-130E Hercules
10315 flying over the Canadian Parliament Buildings
at Ottawa, Ontario. *CAF Official*

Above: A De Havilland Beaver of the Royal Netherlands Air Force pictured at Soesterberg in July 1968. *Aviation Photo News*

Below: A Douglas C-47A transport of the Japanese Maritime Self Defence Force. Hundreds of C-47s remain in service with about 50 air forces throughout the world. *P. Keating, Aviation Photo News*

Above: A Hawker Hunter T7 side-by-side dual-control trainer of 299 OCU, RAF Chivenor, Devon, photographed in September 1970.

Aviation Photo News

Below: A Firestreak missile-armed BAC Lightning T4 side-by-side dual-control trainer of 65 Squadron lands at RAF Coltishall, Norfolk, in June 1971.

Peter R. March

BAC Canberra TT18 WK123 of the Fleet
Requirements Unit, Hurn, shows off its underwing-
mounted Rushton high-speed towed targets as it flies
near the Isle of Wight. *Peter R. March*

Above: Folland Gnat T1s of the famous Red Arrows aerobatic team of the RAF line up on the runway ready to make a steam take-off.

Right above: Looking as though it has had an argument with someone's garden fence, the Beech RU-21D is in fact fitted with an extensive antenna array and was employed on electronic reconnaissance missions in Vietnam. *Beech*

Right: A North American Harvard of 4 (Active Citizen Force) Squadron, South African Air Force, from Zwartkop, pictured at Rand Airport in 1970. *Aviation Photo News*

Westland Whirlwind HAR10s XP343R and XP405D of the Central Flying School hover over Lake Bala, North Wales, during a survival training mission in August 1969.   *Ministry of Defence*

A dayglo-marked Sikorsky CH-34 of the Federal German Navy shows its paces at the Third International Helicopter Rescue Meeting at RAF Thorney Island, Hants, in June 1969.

Aviation Photo News

Above: A Kaman HH-43B Huskie fire-fighting
helicopter of Detachment 2 of the 40th Aerospace
Rescue and Recovery Wing at Upper Heyford in 1970.
Peter R. March

Below: Westland Wessex HAS3 XS121 of 737
Squadron, Fleet Air Arm, photographed at Yeovilton,
Somerset, in September 1970.   *Peter R. March*

Above: Westland Sea King HAS1 XV649 of 737 Squadron, FAA, passes over Portland Bill lighthouse as it heads out to sea from its home base on June 17, 1971. *Peter R. March*

Below: Pumas and the Needles. Three Westland Aerospatiale Pumas from RAF Odiham, Hants, passing the Isle of Wight during a training sortie in 1971.

Peter R. March

Above: Bell CUH-1H Iroquois 118105 of the
Canadian Armed Forces goes into action during a
fire-fighting exercise at CFB Uplands, Ottawa, Ontario.
CAF official

Right: A Sikorsky S-61N of British European Airways
Helicopter Division acts as an aerial crane while
hovering near a power station.

Short Skyvan Series 3 G-AWCS of South West
Aviation pictured in August 1968 during a flight from
its base at Exeter Airport.   *Gazelle Film Productions*

The Canadair CL-215 water-bomber prototype,
CF-FEU-X, makes its first drop tests at Lac Simon,
Quebec, in 1968.   It was able to pick up and release
a maximum of 12,000lb of water on each fire-fighting
sortie.   *Canadair*

Say it with flowers.   Boeing 737 N571GB in Aloha's
colourful Funbird livery during a pre-delivery test flight
ın February 1969.   *Boeing*

Concorde by night; 002, with fin and fuselage
protected by acoustic blankets, re-enters the hangar at
Filton, Bristol, on September 25, 1968, after
completion of a series of powerplant ground-running
tests. *BAC*

Left above: Trident 3 G-AWYZ, first of BEA's fleet of 26, cruising over the coast of Cyprus in 1971. *BEA*

Left: BAC One-Eleven 432 G-AXMU in service with Laker Airways at Gatwick in late 1969, pending delivery to Bahamas Airways (since wound up) whose livery it wears. *Jonathan Bingham*

Above: Hawker Siddeley HS748 Model 209 PI-C1018 makes a test flight from Woodford, Cheshire, before delivery to Philippine Air Lines for use on that operator's inter-island routes.
Hawker Siddeley Aviation

Splendid study of the first production Britten-Norman
Trislander, wearing a non-standard version of Aurigny
Air Service's livery, over the Needles lighthouse, just off
the Isle of Wight.   *Ian Mitchell via Britten-Norman*

Above: Britten-Norman Islander G-AWBZ, one of
Aurigny Air Service's earliest Islanders, awaits
passengers at Eastleigh Airport, Southampton, in 1971.
Peter R. March

Below: Lockheed L-188C Electra SE-FGA of the
now defunct Swedish airline Falconair in its stylish
yellow and white colour scheme.
Aviation Photo News

Left above: Hawker Siddeley Trident 1E-110 G-AVYC of Northeast Airlines breaks formation with the camera ship during a photographic sortie early in 1971.
Hawker Siddeley Aviation

Left: Douglas DC-3C CF-JRY named *Arctic 7* and painted in an eye-catching colour scheme which earned it the nickname 'The Psychedelic Dak' pictured at de Havilland Canada's Downsview Airport, Ontario, in June 1970. *Kenneth Allen*

Above: The first Lockheed TriStar airbus gleams in the sun at Lockheed's Palmdale, California, flight test facility from where it made its first flight on November 16, 1970. *Lockheed*

Above: First of Lufthansa's 365-passenger Boeing 747-30 jumbo jets, D-ABYA, flying over the snow-covered mountains of Washington State during a pre-delivery test flight in 1970. *Boeing*

Right above: McDonnell Douglas DC-8 Super 62 N1805 of Braniff International. The Super 62 is the ultra-long-range version of the Super Sixty series. *McDonnell Douglas*

Right: Another example of the immortal Douglas DC-3, this time CF-HTH of the Canadian operator Nordair. *Aviation Photo News*

Rolls-Royce's Avro Vulcan flying test bed seen in 1971
when it was undertaking engine and intake anti-icing
tests of the belly-mounted Olympus 593 engine,
powerplant of the Concorde SST.   Beneath the nose
is a water spray grid.   *Rolls-Royce*

Wien Consolidated Airlines Boeing 737-293 N461GB
making its first flight in April 1968, escorted by Boeing's
Canadair Sabre V chase plane, N8686F.   *Boeing*

Beech 99 N850SA of Shawnee Airlines, Herndon Airport, Orlando, Florida, which acquired a fleet of these turboprop feeder liners for scheduled commuter services linking Orlando with several other important centres in Florida. *Beech*

Above: Boeing 747-31 N91307 of Trans World Airlines leaves the jumbo jet terminal at London Heathrow Airport in 1970.

A. T. Halse, Aviation Photo News

Below: Douglas DC-7 N4889C of the Atlanta Skylarks, Georgia's Flying Country Club.

Aviation Photo News

A 1969 model Bolkow Bo208C Junior III lightplane
seen during a brief demonstration visit to the Flairavia
Flying Club at Biggin Hill, Kent, early in 1969.
Richard Riding

Piper Cherokee Arrow 200 N7626J, a 1969 model
with a 200hp fuel-injection Lycoming 10-350-CIC
engine giving all-round improvement in performance
over the 180hp Arrow. *Piper*

The veteran Comper Swift G-ACTF, *The Scarlet Angel,*
peels off after formating with the Cessna 172 camera
plane during a photographic sortie over Warwickshire.
Air Portraits

A Helio Courier finished in the eye-catching polka-dot
livery used by Comstol Air Transit on its Air Bear and
Air Squaw air taxi services to ski resorts high in the
Sierra Nevada mountains of California. *Comstol*

1939-vintage Chilton DW1A G-AFSV, the only DW1A
ever built, shows off its colourful livery during a
sortie from Wycombe Air Park in 1969 piloted by
Sqn Ldr 'Manx' Kelly. *Air Portraits*

Above: Another Comper Swift, this time G-ABTC pictured with its wings folded at Blackbushe aerodrome in April 1971. *Tony Leigh*

Below: De Havilland 88 Comet G-ACSS *Grosvenor House*, winner of the England-Australia International Air Race of 1934, at its present home at Old Warden, Beds. *Stuart Howe*

Bücker 131 Jungmann HB-URH seen in a typical
Swiss setting while visiting the airfield at Sarnen.
Michael Stroud

Above: Under summer skies. The immaculate veteran de Havilland Hornet Moth G-AELO basks in the sun at Biggin Hill International Air Fair in June 1970. *Peter R. March.*

Below: Another famous marque of de Havilland lightplane, the immortal Tiger Moth biplane, exemplified by the dazzle-painted G-ANDP of Ards Tiger Group. *Peter R. March*

Beagle Pup 2 G-AXID of Southern Aero Club Pashley Ltd flies over Shoreham, Sussex, during a sortie from the local airfield in 1971.   *Southern Aero Club*

Above: Pictured at Shoreham in September 1971, HB-NAA was the first production Pup 150 originally delivered to the Swiss Aero Club about two years earlier. *Tony Leigh*

Below: Another Beagle Pup 150, G-AXHO, photographed at Bristol Lulsgate Airport. From the Pup was developed the Bulldog training aircraft. *Peter R. March*

Above: A Cessna FA150 lightplane. By 1972 well over 15,000 examples of the Model 150 had been built, making it the world's most-produced two-seat lightplane. *Peter R. March*

Below: Miles Messenger 2A G-AKBO at Blackbushe in February 1971. The M38 Messenger was first produced during WWII for light liaison duties, one example being used by General Montgomery.
Tony Leigh